Ms. Blau Screams Loud!

I0108321

Peter ✓✓
Joanna ✓✓
Anthony ✓
Kenneth ✓✓
Gina ✓✓
Marcos ✓
Jennie ✓✓
Dominic ✓
Linda ✓✓
Ashley ✓✓
Edgar ✓
Bethany ✓
Denise ✓
Fatima ✓

Written by:
Glen S. Hoffman

This book is dedicated to everyone who has memories of a real mean teacher that made them feel unimportant, dumb, and occasionally made them cry. As a child, I struggled with reading and faced more humiliation than support by a couple of my teachers. However, there were supportive teachers who convinced me to believe in myself and explained how perseverance pays off. These teachers made a difference in my life and I try to do the same with my own students. Inspiration with kind words is a priceless gift we can all give to one another!

Special thanks to Eugene Ring and Rosalia Villalobos for their advice and editing expertise with this book...

My name is Dominic and I'm in Ms. Blau's third grade class.

☹
―――――

Peter ✓✓✓
Joanna ✓✓
Anthony ✓
Kenneth ✓✓
Gina ✓✓
Marcos ✓
Jennie ✓✓
Dominic ✓
Linda ✓✓
Ashley ✓✓
Edgar ✓
Bethany ✓
Denise ✓
Fatima ✓

Ms. Blau is really fat and mean. And the hairy mole on her chin is quite scary when she screams.

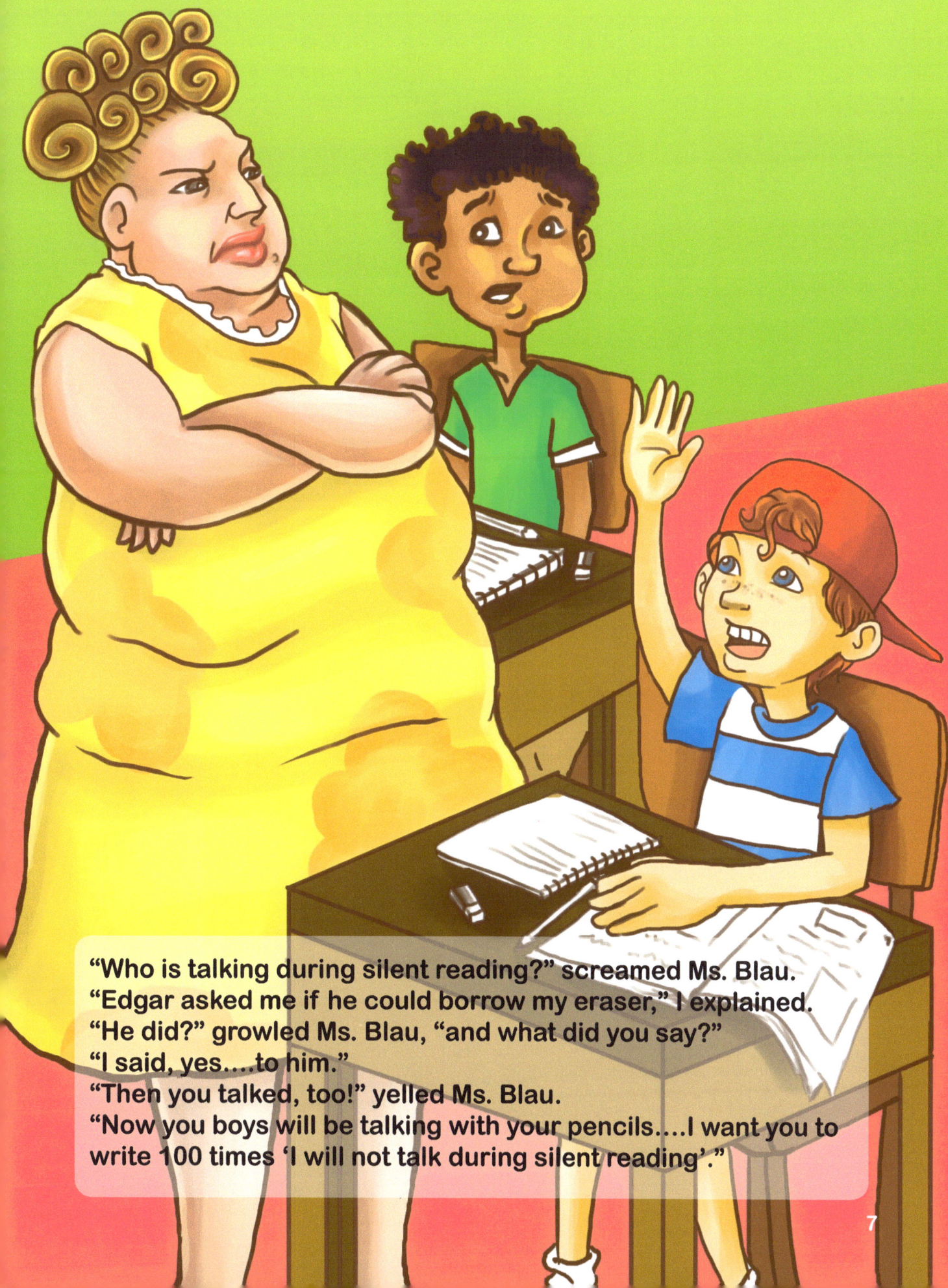

"Who is talking during silent reading?" screamed Ms. Blau.
"Edgar asked me if he could borrow my eraser," I explained.
"He did?" growled Ms. Blau, "and what did you say?"
"I said, yes....to him."
"Then you talked, too!" yelled Ms. Blau.
"Now you boys will be talking with your pencils....I want you to write 100 times 'I will not talk during silent reading'."

That same morning, a new girl named Linda arrived at our classroom. She looked a little frightened when she saw Ms. Blau. But Ms. Blau put on a phony smile and pretended to be sweet.

"Where should I put little Linda?" asked Ms. Blau.
Then she told Gina to move to the back, so Linda could sit in front.
"I can't see the blackboard from way back there!" cried Gina.
"You're like a giant compared to Linda, so she's sitting in front!"
"But my glasses don't let me see that far away," Gina whimpered.
"Then you need stronger glasses....now get moving!"

Soon it was math time and Ms. Blau asked for some volunteers to do a problem at the blackboard. I raised my hand real high, but I didn't say, "Oogh, oogh!" because Ms. Blau hates that.

Ashley's problem was correct, but not Marcos.
"Oh no!" Ms. Blau exclaimed, "this is a disgrace, Marcos...tomorrow you will practice subtraction during recess!"
"Yes, Ms. Blau," said Marcos quietly.

I was correct, but Linda's answer was wrong.
"You made a mistake Linda!" Ms. Blau said.
"Oops!" said Linda.

"Did they teach you how to subtract at that other school?"
"Yes," Linda replied.

"Then how come you got it wrong?"
"Oops!" said Linda once more.

"Stop saying oops!" cried Ms. Blau.
"Yes, Teacher," answered Linda.

"It's Ms. Blau, not Teacher!" snapped Ms. Blau.
"Oops!" Linda accidently said again.

"Get to that corner now!" thundered Ms. Blau.

As Linda stood in the corner of the classroom, everyone smiled at each other. It was so funny watching Ms. Blau turn red like a tomato every time Linda said, "Oops!" Finally, third grade was becoming fun.

A girl named Jennie asked, "Can I please go to the restroom?"

"Why didn't you go at recess?" asked Ms. Blau.

"I forgot." said Jennie.

"Well, you should remember things like that," said Ms. Blau.

"I really need to go!" whined Jennie.

"Is this an emergency?"

"Yes!" Jennie cried.

"Oh, it's always an emergency with you," said Ms. Blau.

"but you're not going this time….so stop asking!"

"She peed in her pants!" shouted Anthony.

"Who peed in their pants?" yelled Ms. Blau.

"Jennie did….there's a puddle under her chair!" Anthony announced.

"Why didn't you tell me it was an emergency?" screamed Ms. Blau.

"I did!" Jennie cried back.

"Class, line up now....we're taking a walk to the restroom....and you honey, are going to wait in the nurse's office 'til your mom arrives with clean clothes or diapers for that matter!" scoffed Ms. Blau.

After we returned, I heard Kenneth and Peter talking.
"They're gonna get it," I said to myself.
"Who's talking," shouted Ms. Blau....."was it you Gina?"
"No, Ms. Blau," Gina replied.
"Then who was it?"
Gina just sat there speechless.
"I want to know now, young lady!" demanded Ms. Blau.
"It was Kenneth and Peter," replied Gina.

Peter ✓✓✓
Joanna ✓✓
Anthony ✓
Kenneth ✓✓
Gina ✓✓
Marcos ✓
Jennie ✓✓
Dominic ✓
Linda ✓✓
Ashley ✓✓
Edgar ✓
Bethany ✓
Denise ✓
Fatima ✓

"Kenneth, were you talking?" asked Ms. Blau.
"Oops!" said Kenneth.

"And you, Peter?"
"Yes," he replied.

"Don't you boys know the rules?"
"Oops!" said Peter.

"What did you say, Peter?"
"Nothing," he replied.

"What did he say, class?"
"Oops!" everyone shouted.

"Is he allowed to say, 'Oops!' in class?"
"No!" we all screamed back.

So Kenneth and Peter had to write a hundred words and their definitions.

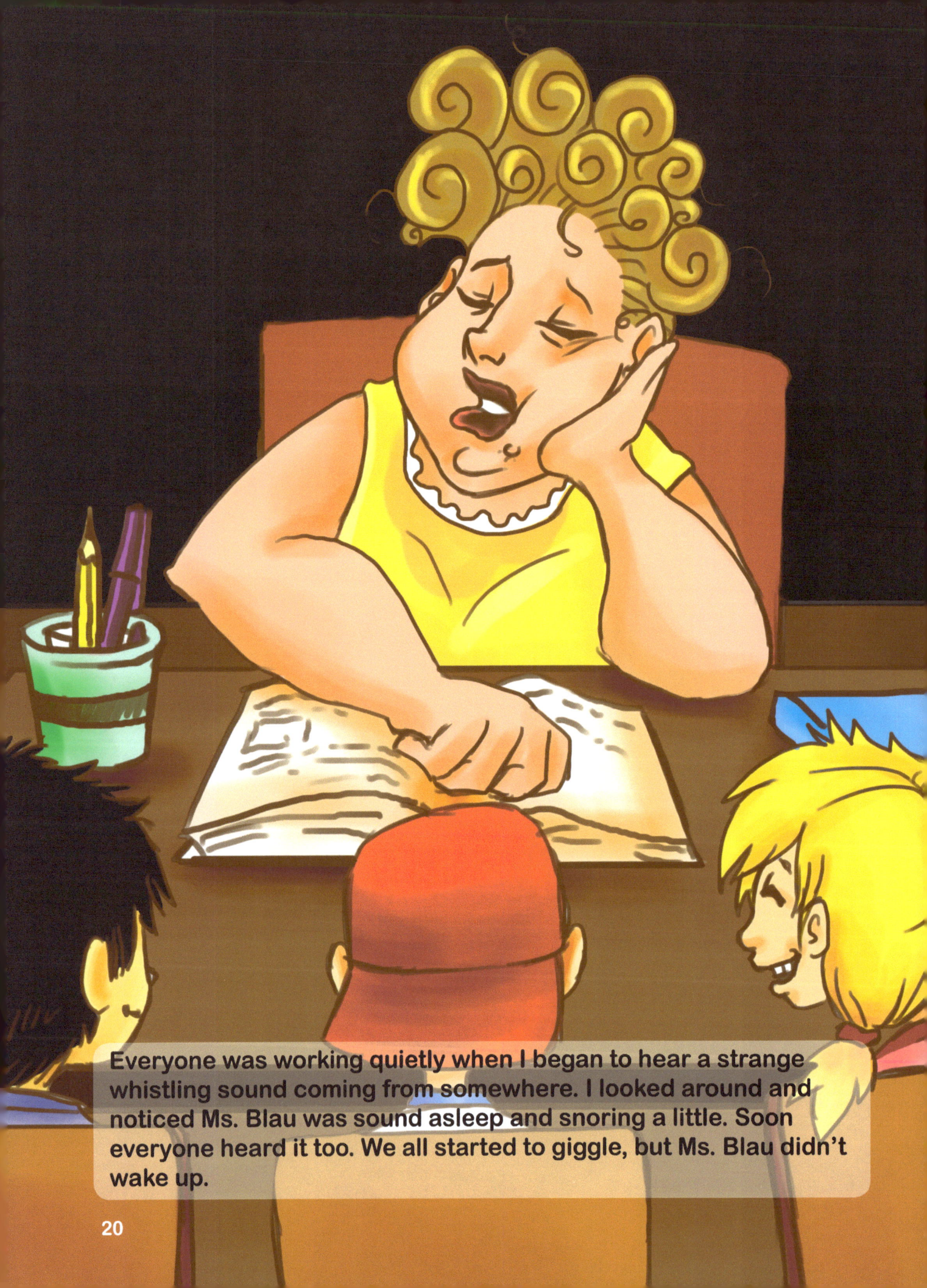

Everyone was working quietly when I began to hear a strange whistling sound coming from somewhere. I looked around and noticed Ms. Blau was sound asleep and snoring a little. Soon everyone heard it too. We all started to giggle, but Ms. Blau didn't wake up.

Bethany went beside Ms. Blau and said,
"I guess the big ole' lion is taking a nap!"

"Don't wake her up or she'll bite your head off,"
said Marcos.

Joanne added, "I'm Ms. Blau and you're all bad
boys and girls!"

Anthony and Edgar made silly faces at her.

Some kids began writing on the blackboard.

Others took out games and blocks from the
closet.

But Ms. Blau kept snoring away.

"Hey, maybe something's wrong...maybe she's sick!" yelled Gina.

Everyone stopped what they were doing and gathered around Ms. Blau.

Fatima got a wet paper towel and put it on Ms. Blau's forehead.

Anthony and Edgar ran to the office for help.

Principal Campbell came running.
"Martha, send for an ambulance, immediately!" he shouted into his walkie talkie.

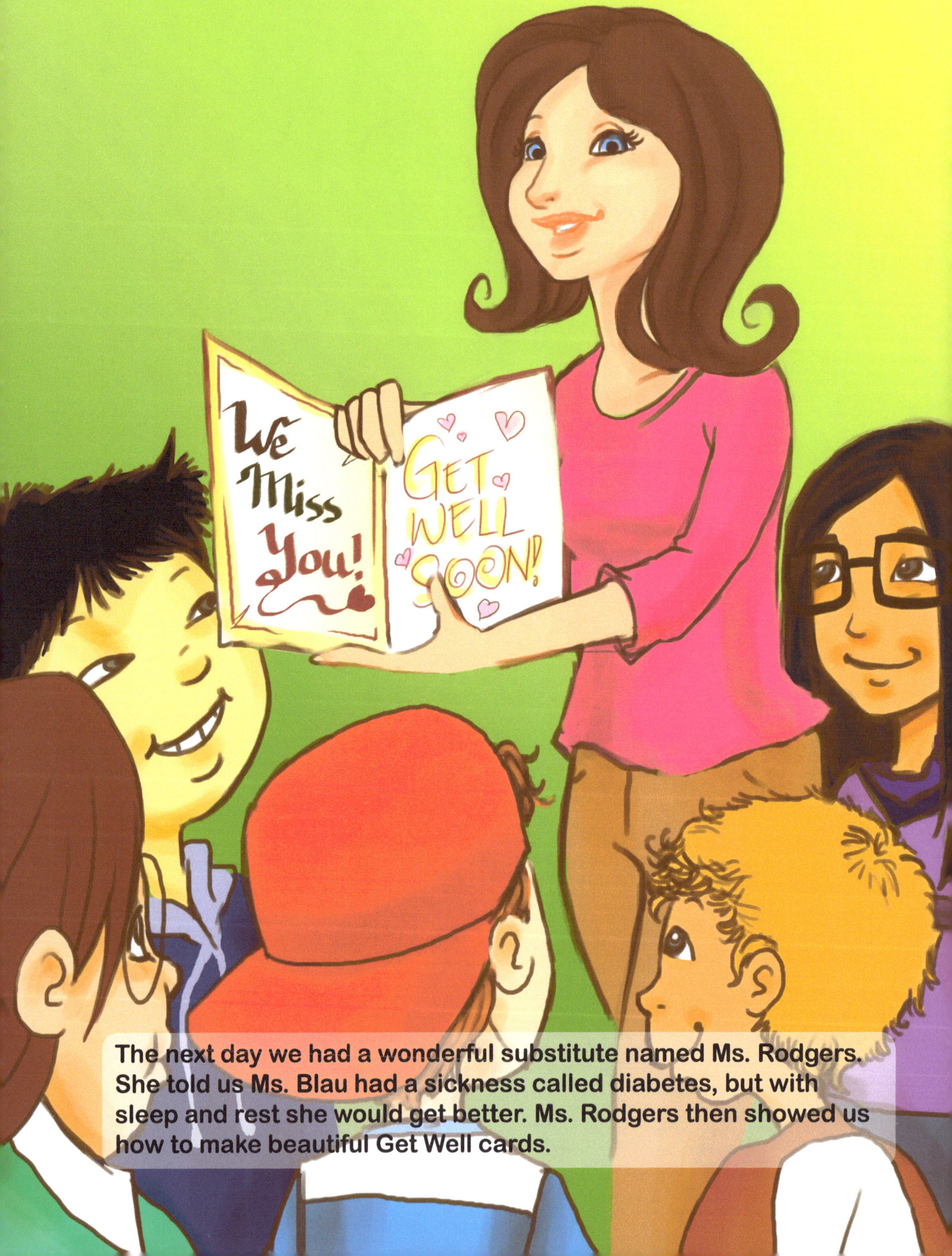

The next day we had a wonderful substitute named Ms. Rodgers. She told us Ms. Blau had a sickness called diabetes, but with sleep and rest she would get better. Ms. Rodgers then showed us how to make beautiful Get Well cards.

SUPER STUDENTS

Peter ✓✓✓✓✓
Joanna ✓✓✓✓
Anthony ✓✓✓✓
Kenneth ✓✓✓✓
Gina ✓✓✓✓
Marcos ✓✓✓✓
Tennie

Be
De
Fati

SUPERBLAU

A week later, Ms. Blau returned. She thanked us for the lovely cards and promised to never scream at us again.

That afternoon, Ms. Blau brought us ice-cream cones.

Principal Campbell came by to visit, so Ms. Blau kindly offered him one.

"Ms. Blau, are you allowed to eat sweets with your diabetes?" he asked.

"Oops!" said Ms. Blau.

"You forgot, Ms. Blau?" he asked.

"Oops!" shouted the whole class.

Then Ms. Blau said, "Oops!" again.

We all started laughing, including Ms. Blau, and everyone started saying "Oops!" over and over again.

Ms. Blau never screams at us anymore. She says I'm becoming a superstar reader and she's proud of me. She often says, "Oops!" and giggles, too. Ms. Blau is now one of my favorite teachers.

"this book belongs to:_____"

www.ingramcontent.com/pod-product-compliance
Lightning Source LLC
Chambersburg PA
CBHW041556040426

42447CB00002B/183